Y0-CAT-170

THE SUN AND THE SOLAR SYSTEM

Nancy Dickmann

WINDMILL
BOOKS

Published in 2019 by **Windmill Books**, an imprint of Rosen Publishing
29 East 21st Street, New York, NY 10010

Copyright © 2019 BROWN BEAR BOOKS LTD

All rights reserved. No part of this book may be reproduced in any form
without permission in writing from the publisher, except by a reviewer.

For Brown Bear Books Ltd:
Text and Editor: Nancy Dickmann
Children's Publisher: Anne O'Daly
Editorial Director: Lindsey Lowe
Design Manager: Keith Davis
Designer and Illustrator: Supriya Sahai
Picture Manager: Sophie Mortimer

Concept development: Square and Circus/Brown Bear Books Ltd

Picture Credits:
Front cover: Supriya Sahai
Interior: iStock: adventtr 13, 28, eucyin 5; NASA: 14, ESA/SOHO 7, Goddard/SDO 16,
Hinode/JAXA/PPARC 10, JPL 4, JPL-Caltech 19, Line (Caltech), Mike/Ed Mierkiewicz
(Univ.Wisconsin-Madison)/Ron Oliversen (NASA-GSFC) 24, SDO 25, SDO/HMI 15, 28–29;
Shutterstock: alexaldo 9, By 22, D1min 20, Andrea Danti 27, Dotted Yeti 21, fzd.it 12,
Sergey Nivens 8, sciencepics 26, 29, Twin Design 16–17.

Key: t=top, b=bottom, c=center, l=left, r=right

Brown Bear Books has made every attempt to contact the copyright holder.
If anyone has any information please contact licensing@brownbearbooks.co.uk

Cataloging-in-Publication Data

Names: Dickmann, Nancy.
Title: The sun and the solar system / Nancy Dickmann.
Description: New York : Windmill Books, 2019. | Series: Space facts and figures |
Includes glossary and index.
Identifiers: LCCN ISBN 9781508195238 (pbk.) | ISBN 9781508195221 (library bound) |
ISBN 9781508195245 (6 pack)
Subjects: LCSH: Sun--Juvenile literature. | Solar system--Juvenile literature.
Classification: LCC QB521.5 D53 2019 | DDC 523.7--dc23

Manufactured in the United States of America

CPSIA Compliance Information: Batch #BS18WM:
For Further Information contact Rosen Publishing, New York, New York at 1-800-237-9932

CONTENTS

WHAT IS A SOLAR SYSTEM?

We live on Earth, but our planet is not alone. It is part of a giant "family" called the solar system.

The solar system is made up of the sun and all the objects that surround it. The sun is a star. It is at the center of the solar system. The solar system has different types of objects, including **planets**, **moons**, **asteroids**, and **comets**.

Asteroid

There are millions of objects in the solar system.

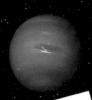
Neptune

Uranus

Saturn

There are probably billions of similar systems in the universe.

Jupiter

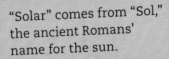
"Solar" comes from "Sol," the ancient Romans' name for the sun.

Mars

Earth is the sixth-largest object in the solar system.

Earth

Venus

Mercury

The sun is the only star in the solar system.

GO FIGURE!

Stars in the solar system: 1
Planets in the solar system: 8
Solar system size: about 18 billion miles (30 billion kilometers) in diameter

OUR SUN

Without the sun, there would be no solar system. This star provides heat and light to all the other objects.

The sun is a giant ball of hot, glowing gas. Compared to Earth, it is absolutely enormous. But compared to other stars, it is average-sized. The objects that surround the sun, such as planets and comets, are much smaller than it is. Jupiter is so big that all the other planets could fit inside it. Even so, 1,000 Jupiters could fit inside the sun.

The moon appears the same size as the sun, but it is much smaller. It looks bigger to us because it is closer.

Size of Earth compared to the sun

The sun makes up more than 99% of the **mass** in the solar system.

(!) NEVER look directly at the sun. It can seriously damage your eyes.

The sun is a type of star called a yellow dwarf.

Solar flare

Planets can be made of gas or rock, but all stars are made of gas.

The sun is one of billions of stars in a **galaxy** called the Milky Way.

GO FIGURE!

Diameter of the sun: 864,000 miles (1,391,473 kilometers)
Volume of the sun: 1,301,019 times Earth's volume
Age of the sun: 4.6 billion years

GRAVITY

The sun has a very important job. Its gravity keeps everything in the solar system from flying off into space.

Everything that has mass has **gravity**. Gravity is a force that attracts objects to each other. The more mass an object has, the stronger its gravity. The sun's gravity can affect objects that are billions of miles away. Gravity keeps objects traveling in paths that loop around the sun.

To get into space, spacecraft must escape Earth's gravity.

Gravity is what makes objects fall down to the ground.

The scientist Isaac Newton developed theories about gravity in the 1600s.

The force of gravity pulls large objects like planets and stars into a ball shape.

Gravity keeps the planets moving in their orbits.

GO FIGURE!

Mass of the sun: 333,060 times Earth's mass
Gravity on sun's surface: 28 times Earth's gravity

INSIDE THE SUN

The sun is made of gas, but it is divided into layers. Each layer is different.

At the center of the sun is the **core**. It is incredibly hot. Outside that are two thick layers called the radiative zone and the convection zone. The **temperature** in these two zones drops as you move outward. The **photosphere** lies outside the convection zone. The chromosphere is outside the photosphere. The outer atmosphere is called the corona. It stretches out into space.

The sun doesn't have a solid surface.

The sun's photosphere is marked by a pattern called granulation.

Energy produced in the sun's core travels outward through the layers.

The photosphere is the layer of the sun that we see.

The corona is much hotter than the photosphere.

GO FIGURE!

Temperature of the core: 28 million °F (15.5 million °C)
Depth of radiative zone: 186,000 miles (300,000 kilometers) thick
Temperature of the photosphere: 10,000 °F (5,540 °C)
Depth of photosphere: 300 miles (500 kilometers) thick
Temperature of the corona: 3.6 million °F (2 million °C)

Chromosphere

Photosphere

Convection zone

Radiative zone

Core

HOW THE SUN SHINES

Powerful reactions take place deep inside the sun. They are nuclear reactions. These reactions produce heat and light.

The sun is mostly made of two gases: hydrogen and helium. Like all materials, these gases are made up of **atoms** that are too tiny to see. In the sun's core, atoms of hydrogen **fuse**, or join together. They make atoms of helium. The process of fusion produces energy. This energy is what makes the sun shine.

Electron

Proton

Helium atom

Neutron

Atoms contain even smaller **particles**. These are protons, neutrons, and electrons.

The sun's energy reaches Earth in the form of heat and light.

Core

It can take hundreds of thousands of years for energy to travel from the core to the outer layers.

Scientists are trying to re-create the sun's fusion on Earth, as a source of energy.

GO FIGURE!

Hydrogen: 70.6% of the sun's mass
Helium: 27.4% of the sun's mass
Protons in a hydrogen atom: 1
Protons in a helium atom: 2

Once the sun has used up most of its hydrogen, it will start to collapse.

SUNSPOTS

The sun shines every day, without fail. But although its light is constant, its surface is always changing.

Dark spots often appear on the surface of the sun. They are called **sunspots**, and they are cooler than the surrounding area. Sunspots are caused by the sun's **magnetic field**. The strength of the magnetic field changes in a regular cycle. The cycle lasts 11 years. Every 11 years, there is a period with very few sunspots.

A large sunspot can be a lot bigger than Earth.

Most sunspots last for several days, although large ones can often last for weeks.

Sunspots usually appear in groups.

The Italian **astronomer** Galileo was one of the first people to study sunspots.

A sunspot can have a "north" or "south" magnetic field, just like the poles of a magnet.

SOLAR FLARES

Sometimes the sun releases massive bursts of energy. These sudden flashes of light are called solar flares.

Like sunspots, **solar flares** are caused by changes in the sun's magnetic field. Their energy reaches Earth in minutes. It can mess up radio and other communication signals. Another type of explosion can be even bigger. This is called a coronal mass ejection. It sends a cloud of magnetized particles into space.

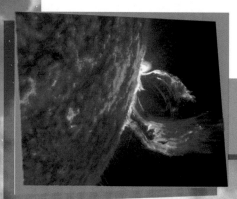

Sometimes solar flares and coronal mass ejections happen at the same time.

A solar flare can last from a few minutes to several hours.

Solar flares are more common during periods where there are many sunspots.

A coronal mass ejection can cause **auroras** that are bigger and more vivid than usual.

Coronal mass ejections can knock out power grids and stop **GPS** from working.

GO FIGURE!

First observation of a solar flare: 1859
Time for light from a solar flare to reach Earth: 8 minutes
Speed of material in a coronal mass ejection: more than 1,000,000 miles (1,610,000 kilometers) per hour

VING THROUGH SPACE

Does the sun move, or stay still? Every day the sun looks like it travels from east to west across the sky.

The sun isn't actually moving—we are! Earth spins around an imaginary line called an **axis**, which goes through its center. This spinning makes it look like the sun is moving. The sun does move, but in a different way. It spins around on its own axis. It also travels through space as the entire Milky Way **rotates**.

Because the sun is made of gas, parts of it rotate at different speeds. It rotates fastest at its equator.

Sun's axis

Sun's equator

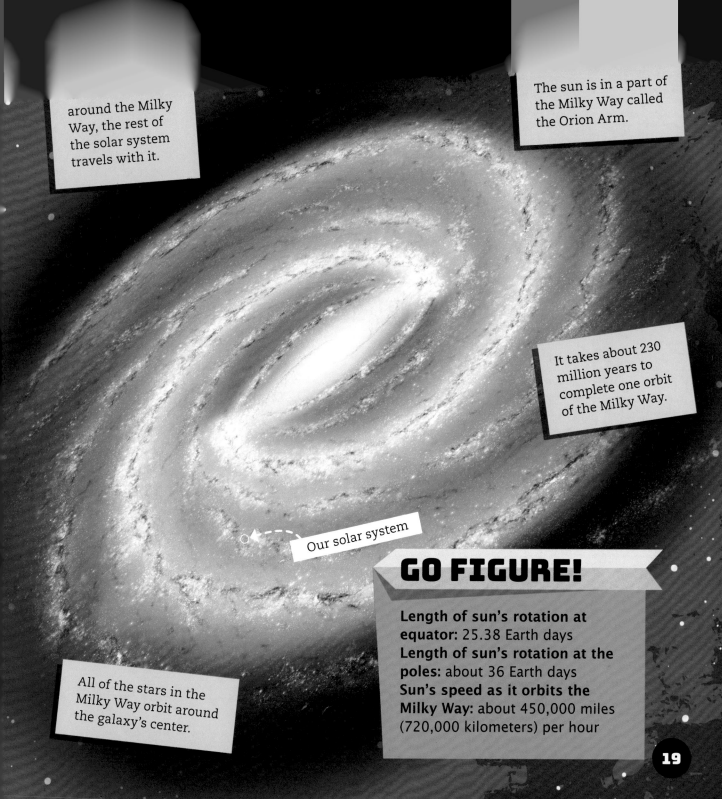

around the Milky Way, the rest of the solar system travels with it.

The sun is in a part of the Milky Way called the Orion Arm.

It takes about 230 million years to complete one orbit of the Milky Way.

Our solar system

All of the stars in the Milky Way orbit around the galaxy's center.

GO FIGURE!

Length of sun's rotation at equator: 25.38 Earth days
Length of sun's rotation at the poles: about 36 Earth days
Sun's speed as it orbits the Milky Way: about 450,000 miles (720,000 kilometers) per hour

PLANETS AND MOONS

After the sun, the largest objects in the solar system are the planets and their moons. They form the inner part of the solar system.

The rocky planets are Mercury, Venus, Earth, and Mars. The gas planets are Jupiter, Saturn, Uranus, and Neptune.

A planet is a large object that travels around the sun. There are eight planets in the solar system. The four closest to the sun are small and rocky. The four farthest are large and made of gas. Six of the planets have at least one moon orbiting them. Earth has one moon, while Jupiter has more than 60.

Mercury
Venus
Earth
Mars
Jupiter
Saturn
Uranus
Neptune

Jupiter and Saturn each have a moon that is larger than Mercury.

Between Mars and Jupiter, there is a band of smaller objects called asteroids.

If you were on one of the outer planets, the sun would look smaller and dimmer than it does from Earth.

Saturn

A moon orbits an object that is not a star, such as a planet or asteroid.

GO FIGURE!

Closest planet to the sun: Mercury, 35,983,125 miles (57,909,227 kilometers) away
Farthest planet from the sun: Neptune, 2,795,173,960 miles (4,498,396,441 kilometers) away
Sunlight on Neptune: about 90 times dimmer than seen from Earth

THE OUTER SOLAR SYSTEM

Beyond the orbit of Neptune, there are trillions of smaller objects. They are too small to be called planets.

The Kuiper Belt is a ring made up of icy bodies. One of them is Pluto. This used to be considered the ninth planet. Then astronomers decided it was actually a **dwarf planet**. The Oort Cloud lies beyond the Kuiper Belt. Its icy objects can sometimes travel into the inner solar system. They become comets, streaking through the sky with long tails of gas and dust streaming out.

A comet travels in a long, looping path around the sun before returning to the Oort Cloud.

Small objects in the Kuiper Belt can also become comets.

Astronomers measure large distances in astronomical units (AU). One AU is the distance from Earth to the sun.

The Kuiper Belt is doughnut-shaped, but the Oort Cloud is probably spherical (shaped like a ball).

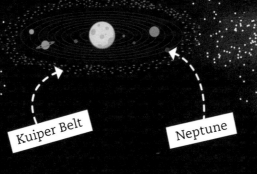

Kuiper Belt

Neptune

Oort Cloud

In the 1990s, astronomers found more objects similar to Pluto. These objects are dwarf planets.

GO FIGURE!

Kuiper Belt distance from the sun: between 30 and 55 AU
Kuiper Belt objects: probably at least 100,000 objects more than 100 miles (62 kilometers) across
Oort Cloud distance from the sun: between 5,000 and 100,000 AU
Oort Cloud objects: probably between 100 billion and 2 trillion

STUDYING THE SUN

The sun is our nearest star. By studying the sun, astronomers can learn more about how stars work.

We can use **telescopes** on Earth to study the sun. The largest of these is the McMath-Pierce Solar Telescope in Arizona. We also use spacecraft to study the sun. Some, like the Solar Dynamics Observatory (SDO) keep track of its activity. They can provide advance warning of coronal mass ejections and other events that might affect Earth.

The McMath-Pierce Solar Telescope in Arizona is the largest solar telescope on Earth.

In 2014, SDO captured images of enormous solar flares.

Solar telescopes can pick up different types of energy coming from the sun, not just light.

Solar flare

GO FIGURE!

McMath–Pierce telescope main mirror:
5 feet 3 inches (1.61 meters) across
SDO launch date: February 11, 2010
SDO size: 14 feet 9 inches (4.5 meters) long
and 7 feet 3 inches (2.22 meters) wide

Many solar telescopes have special filters to keep the sun's light from damaging them.

THE FUTURE OF THE SUN

The sun is very old, but it will not last forever. At some point, it will run out of the hydrogen fuel that keeps it going.

Like all stars, the sun burns fuel. As it uses the fuel up, the core will shrink and the sun will grow brighter. Eventually, the core will collapse. The sun's outer layers will swell out. It will become a type of star called a red giant. Eventually the outer layers will drop off. The sun will turn into a small, bright star called a white dwarf.

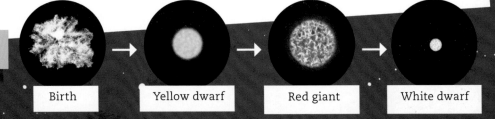

LIFE CYCLE OF THE SUN

Birth → Yellow dwarf → Red giant → White dwarf

The sun is getting very slightly brighter as it uses up its fuel.

In its red giant phase, the sun will swallow up Mercury and Venus, and probably Earth, too.

Stars that are much bigger than the sun end in a huge explosion called a supernova.

As a white dwarf, the sun will slowly cool off over a period of billions of years.

As the sun heats up, it will make Earth's oceans boil away.

GO FIGURE!

Age of the sun: 4.5 billion years
Time until fuel begins to run out: about 4-5 billion years
Time the sun will spend as a red giant: about 120 million years
The sun as a white dwarf: about the size of Earth but with half of the sun's current mass

QUIZ

Try this quiz and test your knowledge of the planets! The answers are on page 32.

1 What is the sun made of?
A. fire
B. gas
C. billions of light bulbs

2 What does the sun's gravity do?
A. it holds everything in the solar system in place
B. it causes planets to form
C. it helps aliens fly

3 What is the center of the sun called?
A. the crust
B. the party zone
C. the core

28

4 What causes dark sunspots on the sun's surface?
A. sunburn
B. pollution
C. changes in the magnetic field

5 During nuclear fusion, what does hydrogen turn into?
A. helium
B. nitrogen
C. ice cream

6 How do coronal mass ejections affect Earth?
A. they make the temperature rise
B. they mess up electronics and communication
C. they make people turn into werewolves

7 What is in the Kuiper Belt?
A. comets, dwarf planets, and other icy objects
B. other stars
C. millions of glitter balls

8 What will happen when the sun begins to run out of fuel?
A. it will have to refuel at a hydrogen station
B. it will turn into a black hole
C. it will swell up into a red giant

29

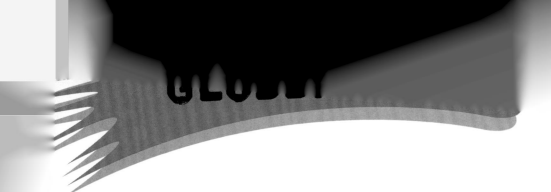
asteroid a large chunk of rock left over from when the planets formed

astronomer person who studies the sun, the planets, and other objects in space

atom the smallest possible unit of an element that cannot be broken down into other substances

aurora shimmering lights sometimes seen in the sky near the north and south poles

axis an imaginary line through the middle of a star, planet, or moon that it spins around

comet rocky, icy object that travels in a long, looping path around the sun

core the center of a star, planet, moon, or some asteroids

dwarf planet object that is too small to be considered a planet, but too big to be an asteroid

energy the ability to do work

fuse to join together and become a single object

galaxy collection of billions of stars held together by gravity

GPS (short for **Global Positioning System**) a network of satellites that allows a receiver on the ground to pinpoint its location

gravity a force that pulls objects together. The heavier or closer an object is, the stronger its gravity, or pull.

magnetic field the area around a star or other object where its magnetism is felt

mass the measure of the amount of material in an object

moon object that orbits a planet or asteroid

nuclear reaction the process in which an atom is either split apart or fused to another atom

orbit the path an object takes around a larger object; or, to take such a path

particle tiny piece of a substance

photosphere one of the outer layers of the sun

planet large, spherical object that orbits the sun or another star

rotate to spin around on a central axis

solar flare a sudden eruption of energy from an area on the sun's surface

sunspot a dark spot that sometimes appears on the surface of the sun

telescope tool used for studying space, which gathers information about things that are far away

temperature how hot or cold something is

FURTHER RESOURCES

Books

Aguilar, David A. *13 Planets: The Latest View of the Solar System.* Washington, DC: National Geographic Kids, 2011.

Mist, Rosalind. *The Solar System.* QEB Publishing, 2014.

Simon, Seymour. *The Sun: Revised Edition.* Collins, 2015.

Taylor-Butler, Christine. *The Sun .* Children's Press, 2014.

Websites

For web resources related
to the subject of this book, go to:
www.windmillbooks.com/weblinks
and select this book's title.

INDEX

Answers to quiz: